SOUTH CAROLINA RULES OF CRIMINAL PROCEDURE 2020
Complete Rules in Effect as of January 1, 2020

Convenient Briefcase Edition Perfect for the Courtroom or Office. Complete Rules in Effect as of January 1, 2020. Rule notes and key case precedents are included.

ISBN: 9781656227560

Peter Edwards, Esq.
South Carolina Legal Publishing, LLC

Table of Contents

I. **Pretrial Matters** 4
    RULE 1. SHERIFF TO FILE AFFIDAVITS ON ARREST 4
    RULE 2. PRELIMINARY HEARINGS 4
    RULE 3. DISPOSITION OF ARREST WARRANTS 5
    RULE 4. MOTIONS IN GENERAL 6
    RULE 5. DISCLOSURE IN CRIMINAL CASES 7
    RULE 6. RULE FOR CHEMICAL ANALYSIS AND CHAIN OF CUSTODY 11
    RULE 7. CONTINUANCES 13
    RULE 8: [RESERVED] 14

II. **Trial** 16
    RULE 13. SUBPOENAS 16
    RULE 14. TRIAL BY JURY 17
    RULE 16. PRESENCE OF ACCUSED AT TRIAL 18
    RULE 17. RESERVATION OF OBJECTIONS 18
    RULE 18. ARGUMENT ON OBJECTIONS 18
    RULE 19. DIRECTED VERDICT 19
    RULE 20. INSTRUCTIONS 20
    RULE 22. ADDRESSING THE JURY 20
    RULE 23. SEPARATION OF JURY 20
    RULE 24. EXPERT TESTIMONY *Deleted* 21

III. **Post Trial Matters** 22
    RULE 28. AFFIDAVIT IN MITIGATION - HOW SUBMITTED 22
    RULE 29. POST TRIAL MOTIONS 22
    RULE 30. PROCESSING AND MAINTAINING BENCH WARRANTS 24

IV. **General Provisions** 25
    RULE 35. TIME 25
    RULE 36. FORMS 25
    RULE 37. APPLICABILITY 25

RULE 38. TITLE AND CITATION 26
RULE 39. RULES REPEALED 26
RULE 40. EFFECTIVE DATE 26
APPENDIX OF FORMS 27
FORMS 27

I. Pretrial Matters

RULE 1. SHERIFF TO FILE AFFIDAVITS ON ARREST

The Sheriff and/or law enforcement officer shall file with the appropriate magistrate the affidavit and/or proof of service on which the arrest is made within five days after the arrest.

Note:

Rule 1 is based upon the language of Criminal Practice Rule 1.

RULE 2. PRELIMINARY HEARINGS

(a) Notice of Right. Any defendant charged with a crime not triable by a magistrate shall be brought before a magistrate and shall be given notice of his right to a preliminary hearing solely to determine whether sufficient evidence exists to warrant the defendant's detention and trial. In the case of bailable offenses, the notice shall be given at the bond hearing. In the case of non-bailable offenses, the notice shall be given no later than would be required if the offense were bailable. Notice shall be given orally and also by means of a simple form providing the defendant an opportunity to request a preliminary hearing by signing the form and returning it to the advising magistrate. In all cases, the request for a preliminary hearing shall be made within ten days after the notice.

(b) Time for Hearing. If the defendant requests a preliminary hearing, the hearing shall be held within ten days following the request. The hearing shall not be held, however, if the defendant is indicted by a grand jury or waives indictment before the preliminary hearing is held. The defendant may appear by counsel or in person or both.

(c) Probable Cause. If probable cause be found by the magistrate, the defendant shall be bound over to the Court of General Sessions. If there be a lack of probable cause, the defendant shall be discharged; but his discharge shall not prevent the State from instituting another prosecution for the same offense.

(d) Conclusion of Hearing. After concluding the hearing the magistrate shall transmit forthwith to the Clerk of the Court his findings together with all papers in the hearing.

(e) Delays. Any delay in the holding of a preliminary hearing shall not be grounds for a delay in the prosecution of the case in the Court of General Sessions.

Note:
Rule 2 is the language of Criminal Practice Rule 9.

RULE 3. DISPOSITION OF ARREST WARRANTS

(a) Transmittal to Clerk. Magistrates, municipal judges, and other officials authorized to issue warrants shall, in all cases within the jurisdiction of the Court of General Sessions, forward to the Clerk of the Court of General Sessions all documents pertaining to the case including, but not limited to, the arrest warrant and bond, within fifteen (15) days from the date of arrest in the case of an arrest warrant and date of issuance in the case of other documents. Transmittal shall be pursuant to procedures now or hereafter promulgated by the Office of South Carolina Court Administration.

(b) Transmittal to Solicitor. The Clerk of the Court of General Sessions shall forward a copy of any arrest warrant received pursuant to paragraph (a) above to the solicitor within two (2) business days from date of receipt from the issuing official.

(c) Action on Warrant. Within ninety (90) days after receipt of an arrest warrant from the Clerk of Court, the solicitor shall take action on the warrant by (1) preparing an indictment for presentment to the grand jury, which indictment shall be filed with the Clerk of Court, assigned a criminal case number, and presented to the Grand Jury; (2) formally dismissing the warrant, noting on the face of the warrant the action taken; or (3) making other affirmative disposition in writing and filing such action with the Clerk of Court.

(d) Extensions of Time. The solicitor may petition the circuit court for an order delaying action on the warrant, as set forth above, for successive ninety (90) day periods if the circuit court specifically finds good cause for such delay for each successive ninety day period.

(e) Record of Proceedings. Any action taken pursuant to paragraphs (a), (b), and (c) above shall be entered in the records of the Clerk of Court pursuant to procedures now or hereafter promulgated by the Office of South Carolina Court Administration.

Note:
Rule 3 is the language of Criminal Practice Rule 6.

RULE 4. MOTIONS IN GENERAL

(a) Form of Motions. An application to the court for an order shall be by motion which, unless made during a hearing or trial in open court with a court reporter present, shall be made in writing, shall state with particularity the grounds therefor, and shall set forth the relief or order sought. The requirement of writing is fulfilled if the motion is stated in a written notice of the hearing of the motion.

(b) Subsequent Applications for Order After Refusal. If any motion be made to any judge and be denied, in whole or in part, or be granted conditionally, no subsequent motion upon the same set of facts shall be made to any other judge in that action. If upon such subsequent motion any order be made, it shall be void.

Note:
Section (a) is the language of Rule 7(b)(1), SCRCP, and Section (b) is the language of Rule 43(1), SCRCP. The last sentence of Section (b) is taken from Circuit Court Rule 60.

RULE 5. DISCLOSURE IN CRIMINAL CASES

(a) Disclosure of Evidence by the Prosecution.

(1) Information Subject to Disclosure.

(A) Statement of Defendant. Upon request by a defendant, the prosecution shall permit the defendant to inspect and copy or photograph: any relevant written or recorded statements made by the defendant, or copies thereof, within the possession, custody or control of the prosecution, the existence of which is known, or by the exercise of due diligence may become known, to the attorney for the prosecution; the substance of any oral statement which the prosecution intends to offer in evidence at the trial made by the defendant whether before or after arrest in response to interrogation by any person then known to the defendant to be a prosecution agent.

(B) Defendant's Prior Record. Upon request of the defendant, the prosecution shall furnish to the defendant such copy of his prior criminal record, if any, as is within the possession, custody, or control of the prosecution, the existence of which is known, or by the exercise of due diligence may become known, to the attorney for the prosecution.

(C) Documents and Tangible Objects. Upon request of the defendant the prosecution shall permit the defendant to inspect and copy books, papers, documents, photographs, tangible objects, buildings or places, or copies or portions thereof, which are within the possession, custody or control of the prosecution, and which are material to the preparation of his defense or are intended for use by the prosecution as evidence in chief at the trial, or were obtained from or belong to the defendant.

(D) Reports of Examinations and Tests. Upon request of a defendant the prosecution shall permit the defendant to inspect and copy any results or reports of physical or mental examinations, and of scientific tests or experiments, or copies thereof, which are within the possession, custody, or control of the prosecution, the existence of which is known, or by the exercise of due diligence may become known, to the attorney for the prosecution, and which are material to the preparation of the defense or are intended for use by the prosecution as evidence in chief at the trial.

(2) Information Not Subject to Disclosure. Except as provided in paragraphs (A), (B), and (D) of subdivision (a)(1), this rule does not authorize the discovery or inspection of reports, memoranda, or other internal prosecution documents made by the attorney for the prosecution or other prosecution agents in connection with the investigation or prosecution of the case, or of statements made by prosecution witnesses or prospective prosecution witnesses provided that after a prosecution witness has testified on direct examination, the court shall, on motion of the defendant, order the prosecution to produce any statement of the witness in the possession of the prosecution which relates to the subject matter as to which the witness has testified; and provided further that the court may upon a sufficient showing require the production of any statement of any prospective witness prior to the time such witness testifies.

(3) Time for Disclosure. The prosecution shall respond to the defendant's request for disclosure no later than thirty (30) days after the request is made, or within such other time as may be ordered by the court.

(b) Disclosure of Evidence by the Defendant.

(1) Information Subject to Disclosure.
(A) Documents and Tangible Objects. If the defendant requests disclosure under subdivision (a)(1)(C) or (D) of this rule, upon compliance with such request by the prosecution, the defendant, on request of the prosecution, shall permit the prosecution to inspect and copy books, papers, documents, photographs, tangible objects, or copies or portions thereof, which are within the possession, custody, or control of the defendant and which the defendant intends to introduce as evidence in chief at the trial.

(B) Reports of Examinations and Tests. If the defendant requests disclosure under subdivision (a)(1)(C) or (D) of this rule, upon compliance with such request by the prosecution, the defendant, on request of the prosecution, shall permit the prosecution to inspect and copy any results or reports of physical or mental examinations and of scientific tests or experiments made in connection with the particular case, or copies thereof, within the possession or control of the defendant, which the defendant intends to introduce as evidence in chief at the trial or which were prepared by a witness whom the defendant intends to call at trial when the results or reports relate to his testimony.

(2) Information Not Subject to Disclosure. Except as to scientific or medical reports, this subdivision does not authorize the discovery or inspection of reports, memoranda, or other internal defense documents made by the defendant, or his attorneys or agents in connection with the investigation or defense of the case, or of statements made by the defendant, or by prosecution or defense witnesses, or by prospective prosecution or defense witnesses, to the defendant, his agents or attorneys.

(c) Continuing Duty to Disclose. If, prior to or during trial, a party discovers additional evidence or material previously requested or ordered, which is subject to discovery or inspection under this rule, he shall promptly notify the other party or his attorney or the court of the existence of the additional evidence or material.

(d) Regulation of Discovery.
(1) Protective and Modifying Orders. Upon a sufficient showing the court may at any time order that the discovery or inspection be denied, restricted, or deferred, or make such other order as is appropriate. Upon motion by a party, the court may permit the party to make such showing, in whole or in part, in the form of a written statement to be inspected by the judge alone. If the court enters an order granting relief following such an ex parte showing, the entire text of the party's statement shall be sealed and preserved in the records of the court to be made available to the appellate court in the event of an appeal.

(2) Failure to Comply With a Request. If at any time during the course of the proceedings it is brought to the attention of the court that a party has failed to comply with this rule, the court may order such party to permit the discovery or inspection, grant a continuance, or prohibit the party from introducing evidence not disclosed, or it may enter such other order as it deems just under the circumstances. The court may specify the time, place and manner of making the discovery and inspection and may prescribe such terms and conditions as are just.

(e) Notice of Alibi.

(1) Notice of Alibi by Defendant. Upon written request of the prosecution stating the time, date and place at which the alleged offense occurred, the defendant shall serve within ten days, or at such time as the court may direct, upon the prosecution a written notice of his intention to offer an alibi defense. The notice shall state the specific place or places at which the defendant claims to have been at the time of the alleged offense and the names and addresses of the witnesses upon whom he intends to rely to establish such alibi.

(2) Disclosure by Prosecution. Within ten days after defendant serves his notice, but in no event less than ten days before trial, or as the court may otherwise direct, the prosecution shall serve upon the defendant or his attorney the names and addresses of witnesses upon whom the State intends to rely to establish defendant's presence at the scene of the alleged crime.

(3) Continuing Duty to Disclose. Both parties shall be under a continuing duty to promptly disclose the names and addresses of additional witnesses whose identity, if known, should have been included in the information furnished under subdivisions (1) or (2).

(4) Failure to Disclose. If either party fails to comply with the requirements of this rule, the court may exclude the testimony of any undisclosed witness offered by either party. Nothing in this rule shall limit the right of the defendant to testify on his own behalf.

(f) Notice of Insanity Defense or Plea of Guilty but Mentally Ill. Upon written request of the prosecution, the defendant shall within ten days or at such time as the court may direct, notify the prosecution in writing of the defendant's intention to rely upon the defense of insanity at the time of the crime or to enter a plea of guilty but mentally ill. If the defendant fails to comply with the requirements of the subdivision, the court may exclude the testimony of any expert witness offered by the defendant on the issue of his mental state. The court may, for good cause shown, allow late filing of the notice or grant additional time to the parties to prepare for trial or make such other order as is appropriate.

(g) Waiver. The court may, for good cause shown, waive the requirements of this rule.

Note:
Rule 5 is the language of Criminal Practice Rule 8. Section (a)(3) has been added to establish time limits for disclosure by the State, and Section (f) has been amended to provide for notification when a defendant intends to enter a plea of guilty but mentally ill.

RULE 6. RULE FOR CHEMICAL ANALYSIS AND CHAIN OF CUSTODY

(a) Report of Chemical Analysis. For the purpose of establishing the physical evidence of a controlled substance or other substance regulated by Title 44, Chapter 53 of the Code of Laws or Rule 61-4 of the Department of Health and Environmental Control, a report signed by the chemist or analyst who performed the test or tests required concerning its nature shall be evidence that the material delivered to him or her was properly tested under procedures approved by the State Law Enforcement Division (SLED), that those procedures are legally reliable and that the material is or contains the substance or substances stated. The report shall be admitted without the necessity of the chemist or analyst personally being present or appearing in court provided:

(1) the report, at a minimum, identifies each item tested, the kind of test or tests conducted on each item, and the chemist's or analyst's conclusion whether the item is or contains a controlled or other regulated substance (to include weight or quantity, if appropriate) in language which can be understood by a juror without the necessity for expert testimony; and,

(2) the report is accompanied by an affidavit of the chemist or analyst who performed the test or tests that:

(A) he or she is certified by SLED as qualified under standards approved by SLED to analyze those substances;

(B) sets forth his or her training and experience as a chemist or analyst, to include the number of times he or she has been qualified as an expert witness and testified in court; and,

(C) he or she conducted the test or tests shown on the report using procedures approved by SLED and that the report accurately reflects his or her opinion regarding the results of those tests.

The defendant or opposing party may object to the introduction of a chemist's or analyst's report at a preliminary hearing, or if no preliminary hearing is held, not later than ten (10) days prior to the trial of the case. If such objection is properly made, the trial judge shall require the chemist or analyst to be present at trial for the purpose of personally testifying.

(b) Certified or Sworn Statement. For the purpose of establishing a chain of physical custody or control of evidence entered under Part A of this Rule, a certified or sworn statement signed by each successive person having custody of the evidence that he or she delivered it to the person stated is evidence that the person had custody and made delivery as stated without the necessity of the person who signed the statement being present in court provided: (1) the statement contains a sufficient description of the substance or its container to distinguish it; and (2) the statement says the substance was delivered in substantially the same condition as when received.

The defendant or his attorney may demand appearance in court of the persons within the chain of custody in the same manner as provided in Section (a).

(c) Disclosure. In a criminal prosecution any reports or papers mentioned in Sections (a) or (b) shall be made available to the defendant or his attorney at the preliminary hearing or if no hearing is held, not later than eleven (11) days prior to the trial of the case.

(d) Waiver of Rights. Nothing in this Rule shall preclude the right of any defendant to obtain an expert chemist or analyst to test a substance in his behalf, provided it is tested under the supervision of the authority having custody of the substance or of SLED. Nothing in this Rule shall preclude the right of any party to introduce any evidence supporting or contradicting reports or papers entered into evidence under this Rule.

Note:
Rule 6 is the language of Criminal Practice Rule 7.

Notes to 1994 Amendment:
This amendment changes Rule 6(a). Under the former rule, all the requirements of this rule were intended to be shown by a single report. This amendment allows the report of the chemist or analyst containing the results of the testing to be a separate document from the affidavit of the chemist or analyst establishing the remaining requirements of this rule. Additionally, the amendment makes minor changes to clarify the meaning of the rule.

RULE 7. CONTINUANCES

(a) Authority to Grant. The chief administrative judge for General Sessions in each circuit shall have exclusive authority to grant continuances of cases scheduled for trial or expected to be called for trial. Continuances may be granted by a presiding judge during a term of court at which he presides only upon written request by counsel, and any order granting a continuance shall be in writing, shall be made only upon a showing of good and sufficient legal cause and shall be filed forthwith with the clerk of court. A continuance granted by a presiding judge cannot extend beyond the next term of court without the approval of the chief administrative judge.

(b) Continuance Because of Absence of Witness. No motion for continuance of trial shall be granted on account of the absence of a witness without the oath of the party, his counsel, or agent to the following effect: the testimony of the witness is material to the support of the action or defense of the party moving; the motion is not intended for delay, but is made solely because he cannot go safely to trial without such testimony; and has made use of due diligence to procure the testimony of the witness or of such other circumstances as will satisfy the court that his motion is not intended for delay.

(1) When a subpoena has been issued, the original shall be produced with proof of service or the reason why not served endorsed thereon or attached thereto; or if lost the same proof shall be offered with additional proof of the loss of the original subpoena.

(2) A party applying for such postponement on account of the absence of a witness shall set forth under oath in addition to the foregoing matter what fact or facts he believes the witness if present would testify to and the grounds for such belief.

(c) Continuance for Good Cause. If other good sufficient cause for continuance is shown, a continuance may be granted by the chief administrative judge for General Sessions Court.

Note:
This replaces Circuit Court Rule 27. The language is substantially the language of Rule 40(c), SCRCP, with additional language regulating the granting of continuances by the chief administrative judge and presiding judges.

RULE 8: [RESERVED]

II. Trial

RULE 13. SUBPOENAS

(a)(1) Issuance of Subpoenas. Upon the request of any party, the clerk of court shall issue subpoenas or subpoenas duces tecum for any person or persons to attend as witnesses in any cause or matter in the General Sessions Court. An attorney, as an officer of the court, may also issue and sign subpoenas or subpoenas duces tecum for any person or persons to attend as witnesses in any cause or matter in the General Sessions Court. The subpoena shall state the name of the court, the title of the action, and shall command each person to whom it is directed to attend and give testimony, or otherwise produce documentary evidence at a specified court proceeding. The subpoena shall also set forth the name of the party requesting the appearance of such witness and the name of counsel for the party, if any. The clerk of court or attorney issuing the subpoena shall utilize a court-approved subpoena form.

(2) Issuance of Subpoena for Personal or Confidential Information About a Victim. A subpoena requiring the production of personal or confidential information about a victim may be served on a third party only by court order. Before entering the order and unless there are exceptional circumstances, the court must require giving notice to the victim so that the victim can move to quash or modify the subpoena or otherwise object.

Note to 2019 Amendment:

The 2019 amendment provides that an attorney is also authorized to issue and sign a subpoena on behalf of a court in which that attorney is licensed to practice. The amendment also makes clear that subpoenas may only be issued to summon a witness to appear or present documentary evidence at a court proceeding. The rule allowing an attorney to issue and sign a subpoena does not apply to any request for a subpoena for a witness located in another state, which is governed by the Uniform Act to Secure the Attendance of Witnesses from Without a State in Criminal Proceedings. See S.C. Code. Ann. §§ 19-9-10 et seq.

(2014). New paragraph (a)(2) adopts a version of the federal rule intended to provide a protective mechanism when the defense subpoenas a third party to provide personal or confidential information about a victim. The amendment requires judicial approval before service of a subpoena seeking personal or confidential information about a victim from a third party.

(b) Service. A subpoena may be served by the sheriff of any county in which the witness may be found, by his deputy or by any other person who is not a party and is not less than eighteen years of age. Service of a subpoena upon an individual may be made by delivering a copy to him personally, or by leaving copies thereof at his dwelling house or usual place of abode with some person of suitable age and discretion then residing therein, or by delivering a copy to an agent authorized by appointment or by law to receive service. Service may be made on any day of the week.

Note:

This rule replaces S.C. Code Ann. Section 19-7-10 (1976) repealed by Act No. 100 of 1985. The language is taken from Section 19-7-10 (1976) and Rule 4(d), 45(c), SCRCP.

Amended by Order dated May 1, 2019.

RULE 14. TRIAL BY JURY

(a) Number of Jurors. A jury shall be composed of twelve members, but at any time before verdict, the parties may agree in writing with the approval of the court that the jury shall consist of any number less than twelve or that a valid verdict may be returned by a jury of less than twelve should the court find it necessary to excuse one or more jurors for any just cause after trial commences.

(b) Waiver. A defendant may waive his right to a jury trial only with the approval of the solicitor and the trial judge.

(c) Protection of Right. In all cases, the trial judge shall ensure that the defendant's rights under the state and federal constitutions to a trial by jury are preserved.

Note:
This replaces Circuit Court Rule 46. The language is based on Rule 23, Fed. R. Crim. P.

RULE 16. PRESENCE OF ACCUSED AT TRIAL

Except in cases wherein capital punishment is a permissible sentence, a person indicted for misdemeanors and/or felonies may voluntarily waive his right to be present and may be tried in his absence upon a finding by the court that such person has received notice of his right to be present and that a warning was given that the trial would proceed in his absence upon a failure to attend the court.

Note:
Rule 16 is the language of Criminal Practice Rule 3.

RULE 17. RESERVATION OF OBJECTIONS

If an objection has once been made at any stage to the admission of evidence, it shall not be necessary thereafter to reserve rights concerning the objectionable evidence.

Note:
This replaces Circuit Court Rule 101. The language is taken from Rule 43(c)(1), SCRCP.

RULE 18. ARGUMENT ON OBJECTIONS

(a) Argument After Ruling. Counsel shall not attempt to further argue any matter after he has been heard and the ruling of the court has been pronounced.

(b) Argument on Objection. No argument shall be made on objections to admissibility of evidence or conduct of trial unless specifically requested by the court.

(c) Interruption of Argument. No attorney shall interrupt another in the course of his argument.

Note:
This replaces the first paragraph of Circuit Court Rule 11. The language is taken from Rule 43(i), SCRCP. Section (c) is taken from Circuit Court Rule 11 regarding interrupting an attorney during argument.

RULE 19. DIRECTED VERDICT

(a) Grounds for Motion. On motion of the defendant or on its own motion, the court shall direct a verdict in the defendant's favor on any offense charged in the indictment after the evidence on either side is closed, if there is a failure of competent evidence tending to prove the charge in the indictment. In ruling on the motion, the trial judge shall consider only the existence or non-existence of the evidence and not its weight.

(b) Defendant's Right to Present Evidence. If a defendant's motion for directed verdict at the close of the evidence offered by the State is not granted, the defendant may offer evidence without having reserved the right.

(c) Submission of Case to Jury. Submission of any charge to the jury shall constitute a denial of any motion for directed verdict previously made by the defendant and not ruled upon.

Note:
This is substantially the substance of Circuit Court Rule 76. The language is taken from Rule 29(a), Fed. R. Crim. P. and the common law.

RULE 20. INSTRUCTIONS

(a) Time for Request. All requests for legal instructions to the jury shall be submitted at the close of the evidence, or at such earlier time as the trial judge shall reasonably direct. All requests must include accurate citation to authorities relied upon.

(b) Objections to Charge. Notwithstanding any request for legal instructions, the parties shall be given the opportunity to object to the giving or failure to give an instruction before the jury retires, but out of the hearing of the jury. Any objection shall state distinctly the matter objected to and the grounds for objection. Failure to object in accordance with this rule shall constitute a waiver of objection.

Note:
This rule replaces Circuit Court Rule 11, and is taken from Rule 51, SCRCP, and Rule 30, Fed. R. Crim. P. (version effective prior to August 1, 1987).

RULE 22. ADDRESSING THE JURY

In arguing before a jury, no attorney shall address or refer to by name or otherwise any member of the jury he is addressing, or otherwise make any personal appeal to any or all members of the jury.

Note:
This is substantially the language of Circuit Court Rule 77.

RULE 23. SEPARATION OF JURY

If it appears that jury deliberations may extend into the night, the court, in its discretion, may order that the jury be taken to suitable sleeping quarters; and on the following morning they shall resume their deliberations. The jury shall be kept together, separately from the public, and as far as practicable, shall at all times, be under the surveillance of bailiffs. Any juror or jurors may be separated for the night from any other juror or jurors. There shall be no unauthorized communication with any member of the jury by any third person and the jury shall be fully protected from any outside influence.

Note:

This replaces Circuit Court Rule 80. The language is taken from Rule 47(c), SCRCP, with minor modifications for clarity.

RULE 24. EXPERT TESTIMONY *Deleted*

Note to 1990 Amendment:

Rule 24 Expert Testimony is taken from Rules 702 to 705 of the Federal Rules of Evidence. The language in paragraph (c) is that of Federal Rule of Evidence 704 prior to its amendment in 1984. The Advisory committee Notes to the Federal Rules of Evidence provide commentary and useful guidance on the use of expert testimony under this Rule.

Note to 1995 Amendment:

This amendment deleted Rule 24, SCRCrimP. Expert testimony is now governed by Rules 702-705 of the South Carolina Rules of Evidence.

III. Post Trial Matters

RULE 28. AFFIDAVIT IN MITIGATION - HOW SUBMITTED

After verdict against him, the defendant shall not be permitted to submit any affidavit to the court which goes to deny matters of fact, but he may submit affidavits as to matters in extenuation or mitigation; provided, they are filed so as to allow the Attorney General or Solicitor a reasonable time to answer them.

Note:
Rule 28 is substantially the language of Criminal Practice Rule 4.

RULE 29. POST TRIAL MOTIONS

(a) Generally. Except for motions for new trials based on after-discovered evidence, post-trial motions shall be made within ten (10) days after the imposition of the sentence. In cases involving appeals from convictions in magistrate's or municipal court, post-trial motions shall be made within ten (10) days after receipt of written notice of entry of the order or judgment disposing of the appeal. The time for appeal for all parties shall be stayed by a timely post-trial motion and shall run from the receipt of written notice of entry of the order granting or denying such motion. The time within which to make the motion shall not be affected by the ending of a term of court or departure of the judge from the circuit, and the circuit judge shall retain jurisdiction of the action for the purpose of hearing and disposing of the motion if not heard and disposed of during the term. Except by consent of the parties, argument on the motion shall be heard in the circuit where the trial or hearing was held. The motion may, in the discretion of the court, be determined on briefs filed by the parties without oral argument.

(b) New Trials Based on After-Discovered Evidence. A motion for a new trial based on after-discovered evidence must be made within one

(1) year after the date of actual discovery of the evidence by the defendant or after the date when the evidence could have been ascertained by the exercise of reasonable diligence. A motion for a new trial based on after-discovered evidence may not be made while the case is on appeal unless the appellate court, upon motion, has suspended the appeal and granted leave to make the motion. Leave of the appellate court is not required if no appeal has been taken or if the appeal has been finally decided in the appellate court.

Note:
The first sentence of this rule is taken from the common law rule that post trial motions be made and heard before the end of the term of court. This rule replaces Criminal Practice Rule 5.

Note to 1990 Amendment:
This amendment deletes reference to Supreme Court Rule 24 which has been repealed. It adds language indicating when a motion for a new trial based on after-discovered evidence may be made in the trial court and when leave from an appellate court must be obtained to make the motion. It modifies the prior practice under Supreme Court Rule 24 by not requiring leave from the appellate court after the conviction has been affirmed.

Note to 1991 Amendment:
This amendment reorganizes Rule 29. It changes prior practice by allowing the parties up to ten (10) days to file post trial motions and by providing the circuit judge jurisdiction to hear and determine these motions despite the end of the term. The amendment also provides flexibility for the circuit judge to determine motions on briefs without oral arguments.

Note to 2011 Amendment:
This amendment places a one year limit on the time to make a motion for a new trial based on after-discovered evidence.

RULE 30. PROCESSING AND MAINTAINING BENCH WARRANTS

(a) Procedure. Subject to the approval of the Chief Justice, the Office of Court Administration shall establish procedures for processing and maintaining bench warrants.

(b) Form. Bench warrants shall be in the form prescribed in these rules and shall require either the signature of the trial judge or the signature of the respective clerk of court at the direction of the trial judge.

(c) Service. It is the continuing duty of the sheriff, and of other appropriate law enforcement agencies in the county, to make every reasonable effort to serve bench warrants and to make periodic reports to the court concerning the status of unserved warrants.

Note:
Rule 30 is the language of Criminal Practice Rule 10.

IV. General Provisions

RULE 35. TIME

In computing any period of time prescribed or allowed by these rules, by order of court, or by any applicable statute, the day of the act, event, or default after which the designated period of time begins to run is not to be included. The last day of the period so computed is to be included, unless it is a Saturday, Sunday or a State or Federal holiday, in which event the period runs until the end of the next day which is neither a Saturday, Sunday nor such holiday. When the period of time prescribed or allowed is less than seven days, intermediate Saturdays, Sundays and holidays shall be excluded in the computation. A half holiday shall be considered as other days and not as a holiday.

Note:
Rule 35 is the language of Rule 6(a), SCRCP.

Adopted by Order dated May 1, 2013.

RULE 36. FORMS

The Supreme Court shall prescribe the content and format of forms required by these rules. The use of the forms as prescribed is mandatory.

Note:
The language of this rule is taken from Rule 84, SCRCP.

RULE 37. APPLICABILITY

These rules shall apply to every trial court of criminal jurisdiction within this State, within the limits of the jurisdiction and the powers of the court provided by law, and the procedure therein shall conform to these rules insofar as practicable. They shall apply insofar as practicable in magistrate's courts, municipal courts, and family courts to the extent they are not inconsistent with the statutes and rules governing those courts. In any case where no provision is made by statute or these rules, the procedure shall be according to the practice as it has heretofore existed in the courts of the State.

Note:
The language of this rule is substantially taken from Rule 81, SCRCP.

RULE 38. TITLE AND CITATION

These rules shall be entitled the South Carolina Rules of Criminal Procedure and shall be cited by rule number and the abbreviation SCRCrimP, i.e., Rule ___, SCRCrimP.

Note:
The language of this rule is taken from Rule 85(c), SCRCP.

RULE 39. RULES REPEALED

All other existing Criminal Practice Rules heretofore adopted are repealed as of the effective date of these South Carolina Rules of Criminal Procedure.

Note:
The language of this rule is taken from Rule 85(c), SCRCP.

RULE 40. EFFECTIVE DATE

These rules shall take effect on September 1, 1988. They govern all proceedings in criminal actions brought after they take effect and also all further proceedings then pending, except to the extent that in the opinion of the court their application in a particular action pending when the rules take effect would not be feasible or would work injustice, in which event the former procedure applies.

Note:
The language of this rule is taken from Rule 86(a), SCRCP.

APPENDIX OF FORMS

    Affidavit of Chemist or Chemical Analyst

    Certificate of Proof of Chain of Physical Custody or Control (Initial Custody)

    Certificate of Proof of Chain of Physical Custody or Control (Subsequent Change of Custody)

    Bench Warrant

    Subpoena in a Criminal Case

    Sentencing Sheet

FORMS

Control No. _____
Print All Information Except Where Signature Is Required

FORM A (Rule 6)

AFFIDAVIT OF CHEMIST OR CHEMICAL ANALYST

RE: Report Number _____

I, _____, am a Chemist employed by _____, and certified by SLED as qualified to perform testing and analysis for controlled substances or other substances regulated by Title 44, Chapter 53 of the Code of Laws or Rule6-4 of the Department of Health and Environmental Control.

I have had _____ years and _____ months experience as a Chemist. During that period, I have been qualified as an expert witness and testified in court no fewer that _____ times. I have received the following training as a Chemist:

(List schools of courses attended; other training received; organizations and honors received.)

I certify that I tested the items listed in the above referenced report using laboratory procedures approved by SLED and that the report accurately reflects my opinion regarding the results of the test of tests performed.

Sworn before me this)	_____
day of _____, 2__.)	(Signature of Chemist of Analyst)
)	
_____)	_____
Notary Public for South Carolina)	(Place)
)	_____
My Commission expires _____)	(Date)

Control No. _____
Print All Information Except Where Signature Is Required

FORM B (Rule 6)

CERTIFICATE OF PROOF OF
CHAIN OF PHYSICAL CUSTODY OR CONTROL
(Initial Custody)

This is to certify that I, _____, am employed by _____ and that on, _____, I seized from _____ pursuant to _____ at or near _____ the following substance(s) or container(s):
(Describe substance or container with sufficient particularity to distinguish it.)
_____

On _____, I made delivery of the above described substance(s) or container(s) to _____ of _____ in substantially the same condition as when I received it.

_____
(Signature)

(Place): _____
(Date): _____

Sworn before me this   )
_____ day of _____ , 2___.___   )
)
_____   )
Notary Public for South Carolina   )
)
My Commission expires _____   )

Control No. _____
Print All Information Except Where Signature Is Required

FORM C (Rule 6)

CERTIFICATE OF PROOF OF
CHAIN OF PHYSICAL CUSTODY OR CONTROL
(Subsequent Change of Custody)

This is to certify that I,   , am employed by   as   and that on
I received   from   of   the following substance(s) of container(s) which were originally seized by   :

(Describe substance or container with sufficient particularity to distinguish it.)
_____

On   , I made delivery of the above described substance(s) or container(s)   of
in substantially the same condition as when I received it.

_____
(Signature)

(Place): _____
(Date): _____

Sworn before me this
_____ day of _____ , 2_____

_____
Notary Public for South Carolina

My Commission expires   _____

STATE OF SOUTH CAROLINA

_____

County of _____   VS.

Court _____
_____

                                                            Warrant/Case No
                                                            _____

To all the Sheriffs, Deputy Sheriffs, Constables and other Peace Officers of the State:

WHEREAS, at the term of the afforested Court, it was among other things ordered that a Bench Warrant should be issued for the arrest of

_____

_____
_____

_____
_____

It is, therefore, ordered that you make diligent search for the above named and take him to the county jail where he will be safely held until he may be brought before this Court, or otherwise discharged by due course of law.

It is further ordered that the county jailer notify the clerk of court immediately, during the normal operating hours of the office of the clerk of court, that the above named is in custody.

WITNESS, the Clerk of Court for the County of
_____

on the _____ day of _____, 20 _____

                                                            _____
                                                                            Clerk of Court

STATE OF SOUTH CAROLINA

County of _____

VS.

_____

======================================
BENCH WARRANT
======================================

Date Served _____

Served by _____

- or -

Date Returned _____

Reason for

Return _____

_____

_____

Bench Warrant No. _____

Issued _____ 20____

Court _____

Home Address _____

_____

Business Address _____

_____

Sex _____ Race _____ DOB _____

Height _____ Weight _____

Eyes _____ Hair _____

Social Security No. _____

UBPOENA IN A CRIMINAL CASE

	COUNTY
SOUTH CAROLINA COURT	
V.	CASE NO.
	SUBPOENA FOR ☐ PERSON ☐ DOCUMENT(S) OR OBJECT(S)

TO:
☐ YOU ARE HEREBY COMMANDED to appear in the above-named court at the place, date, and time specified below to testify in the above-entitled case.

PLACE	COURTROOM
	DATE AND TIME

☐ YOU ARE ALSO COMMANDED to bring with you the following document(s) or object(s).
LIST DOCUMENT(S) OR OBJECT(S)

This subpoena shall remain in effect until you are granted leave to depart by the court or by an officer acting on behalf of the court.	
CLERK OF COURT	DATE
(BY) DEPUTY CLERK	
THIS SUBPOENA IS ISSUED UPON APPLICATION OF THE: ☐ SOLICITOR ☐ DEFENDANT	NAME AND ADDRESS OF ATTORNEY or DEFENDANT (IF PRO SE/SELF REPRESENTED)

PROOF OF SERVICE

SERVED	DATE	PLACE	
SERVED ON (PRINT NAME)			MANNER OF SERVICE
SERVED BY (PRINT NAME)			TITLE

DECLARATION OF SERVER

I certify that the forgoing information contained in the Proof of Service is true and correct.

Executed on

_____
SIGNATURE OF SERVER

ADDRESS OF SERVER

STATE OF SOUTH CAROLINA

COUNTY OF   IN THE COURT OF GENERAL SESSIONS

STATE   INDICTMENT/CASE#:   -GS-   -

VS.   AW#: (   )
                                                    Date of Offense: (   )
                                                    S.C. Code §: (   )
                                                    CDR Code #: (   )

AKA: Sex: Age:
Race: SS#:
DOB:
Address:
City, State, Zip:
DL# _____ *   SID#
*CDL Yes ☐ No ☐   CMV Yes ☐ No ☐   Hazmat Yes ☐ No ☐   SENTENCE SHEET

In disposition of the said indictment comes now the Defendant who was   ☐ CONVICTED OF or ☐ PLEADS
TO:

☐ In violation of §   of the S.C. Code of Laws, bearing CDR Code #
☐ NON-VIOLENT   ☐ VIOLENT   ☐ SERIOUS   ☐ MOST SERIOUS   ☐ Mandatory GPS   ☐ §17-25-45
                                                        (CSC w/minor 1st or CSC w/minor 3rd)   (def.'s initials)
The charge is: ☐ As indicted,   ☐ Lesser Included Offense,   ☐ Defendant Waives Presentment to Grand Jury.
The plea is: ☐ Without Negotiations or Recommendation,   ☐ Negotiated Sentence,   ☐ Recommendation by the State.
ATTEST:

_____   _____   _____
Solicitor   SC Bar #   Defendant   Attorney for Defendant   SC Bar #

WHEREFORE, the Defendant is committed to the ☐ State Department of Corrections ☐ County Detention Center,
for a determinate term of _____ days/months/years or ☐ under the Youthful Offender Act not to exceed _____ years
and/or to pay a fine of $ _____ ; provided that upon the service of _____ days/months/years and or payment
of $ _____ ; plus costs and assessments as applicable*; the balance is suspended with probation for _____
months/years and subject to South Carolina Department of Probation, Parole and Pardon Services standard conditions of probation, which are
incorporated by reference.
☐ CONCURRENT or ☐ CONSECUTIVE to sentence on:
☐ The Defendant is to be given credit for time served pursuant to S.C. Code §24-13-40 to be calculated and applied SCDOC.
☐ The Defendant is to be placed on Central Registry of Child Abuse and Neglect pursuant to S.C. Code §17-25-135.
☐ The Defendant is to report to the Department of Corrections.

Pursuant to 18 U.S.C. Section 922, it is unlawful for a person convicted of a violation of Section 16-25-20 or 16-25-65 (Domestic Violence) to ship, transport, possess, or receive a firearm or ammunition.

                            SPECIAL CONDITIONS:
☐ RESTITUTION: ☐ Deferred   ☐ Def. Waives Hearing   ☐ Ordered   PTUP   ☐

Total: $ _____ plus 20% fee: $ _____   days/hours Public Service Employment

Payment Terms: Obtain GED ☐

☐ Set by SCDPPPS

Attend Voc. Rehab. Or Job Corp.

May serve W/E beginning
Substance Abuse Counseling ☐
Random Drug/Alcohol Testing ☐
Fine may be pd. in equal consecutive weekly/monthly
pmts. of $ Beginning
$ Paid to Public Defender Fund
Other:

Recipient:
*Fine: $
§14-1-206 (Assessments 107.5%) $
§14-1-211 (A)(1)(Conv. Surcharge) $100 $
§14-1-211 (A)(2)(DUI Surcharge) $100 $
§56-5-2995 (DUI Assessment) $12 $
§56-1-286 (DUI Breath Test) $25 $
Proviso (Public Def/Probation) $500 $
§14-1-212 (Law Enforce. Funding) $25 $
§14-1-213 (Drug Court Surcharge) $150 $
§50-21-114 (BUI Breath Test Fee) $50 $
§56-5-2942(J) (Vehicle Assessment) $40/ea $
3% to County (if paid in installments) $

TOTAL $

☐ Appointed PD or appointed other counsel,
Proviso requires $500 be paid to Clerk
during probation and shall be collected before
any other fees.

Presiding Judge
Judge Code:
Sentence Date

Clerk of Court/Deputy Clerk
Court Reporter:
SCCA/217 (04/2018)

www.ingramcontent.com/pod-product-compliance
Lightning Source LLC
Chambersburg PA
CBHW080817220526
45466CB00011BB/3591